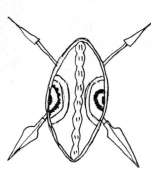

KENYA, JAMBO!

**For the curious, the adventuresome, travelers young and old,
and to those who made it possible:**

Photographers:

Mohamed Amin/Camerapix
Katherine Perrow Klyce
James Paul McCauley
Betty Robinson
Linda Grisham Smith
Allan J. Wade
Frank Hawes Wesson
Rebecca Webb Wilson

Others:

The staff of Friends World College, especially Dr. Robert A. Leonard and Martin Barnes; Douglas Archard, Political Counselor, American Embassy, Khartoum, Sudan; Kilonzo Kiilu and family, Machakos, Kenya; Timothy C. Duffy; Evans and Regina Okuth; Susan Robinson; Lisa Snowden; and Mary Byrd and Gretchen Meriwether Schas.

Artists:

Claire Ackerman, Hilary Askenase, John Bontatibus, Molly Borum, Jay Curtis, Beau Davidson, Jeff Davis, Edward De Barbieri, Elizabeth Entman, Martin Gahbauer, Sam Hall, Bink Hare, Paul Hess, Thomas Hewgley, Susan Jewett, Nduku Kilonzo, Davey Larson, Jackie Lavenbein, Geneine Lindsay, Mathilde McLean, Bill Mealor, William Moore, Ndinda Musuli, Clay Nichol, Peter Pettit, Scott Poitevent, Rob Pope, Grace Pritchard, Jay and Wesley Robinson, Nelson Rockwood, Jill Schoenblum, Logan Schulze, Ronnie Shaw, Harriet Snowden, Hunter Stratton, Josh Tom, Micah Vo, Caitlin Weeks, Luke Wilkens-Minto, Jennie Wolff, Judy Woloshen, Matthew Wu, Andy Young, and their schools, Bear Creek Elementary/Houston, Foote/New Haven, Isidore Newman/New Orleans, Katheka Kai Primary/Machakos, Presbyterian Day/Memphis, University School/Nashville, and Worthington Hooker/New Haven.

Redbird Press, Inc.
P.O. Box 11441
Memphis, TN 38111

Library of Congress Catalog Card Number: 88-63987
ISBN 0-9606046-5-0
First edition, first printing—September 1989

Printed in Hong Kong
by South Sea International Press Ltd.

KENYA, JAMBO!

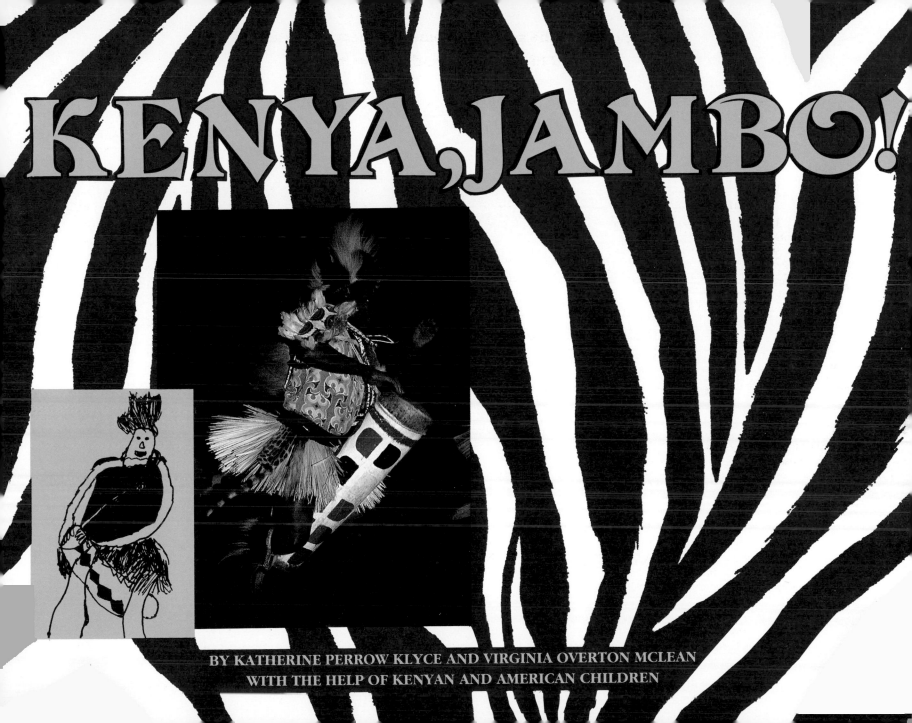

BY KATHERINE PERROW KLYCE AND VIRGINIA OVERTON MCLEAN
WITH THE HELP OF KENYAN AND AMERICAN CHILDREN

The pocket knife and compass were in, but Robert's canteen would not fit. Our packs were crammed with the things we imagined we'd need. We were prepared for snakes dangling from trees in hot tangled jungles, roaring lions and crocodile-infested rivers, strange people with poisoned arrows, a yet-uncharted Africa, the "dark continent."

Our parents were taking us there, to a country called Kenya. I'm
ten years old; my brother is five. We were excited and a little afraid.

Some places are so different from what you
expect that you can hardly believe they're real,
even when you see them with your own eyes.
Nairobi is such a place.

Nairobi is a big, modern city. It's the capital of Kenya, and it's not in the jungle. It sits right in the middle of a huge field that seems as big as the state of Kansas.

Nairobi has all the things I'm used to back home. All kinds of people live there: Africans, Asians, Arabs, and Europeans. There are skyscrapers, shopping malls, and sports stadiums. People ride in cars and on buses, and there are rush hour traffic jams. Kids watch TV and listen to pop music.

The signs are even in English, so I can read them. That's because people from England came here to live about a hundred years ago and brought along their language. It's one of the official languages. In Kenya they have two. The other language is Swahili. It is a mixture of an ancient African language and Arabic, brought by Arab traders in the 8th century. The first word of Swahili I learned was *jambo*. It means hello.

Most Kenyans' first language, though, is the language of their tribe. A tribe is an ethnic group. Each has its own language, customs, beliefs, and way of dressing.

Just like my country, Kenya is made up of many different groups of people. In cities, people from different tribes and different religions live together, and it's hard to tell who's a member of what group. But in the country people live only with their own tribe.

TURKANA

LUO

POKOT

BOK

How a person lives in the country depends on whether he's a member of a tribe that farms or a tribe that herds animals. In Kenya that makes a big difference.

Farmers, like the people of the Kikuyu and the Akamba tribes, live in houses with thatched or tin roofs.

Some work on big farms and grow coffee or tea to sell around the world. Most, however, live on small farms and grow food like corn, tomatoes, and peas to eat or to sell in their local market.

The women cook on an open fire, like a campfire, and roast corn right on the hot coals. It tastes sweet and crunchy when it's roasted this way, and, on some nights, the whole country seems to smell like popcorn.

Farmers' clothes are a lot like mine, but usually only boys wear slacks and shorts. Girls wear dresses, or t-shirts and long scarves wrapped around their waists to make skirts. Some women tie bright colored scarves around their heads.

Others fix their hair in one of the many styles of Swahili braids.

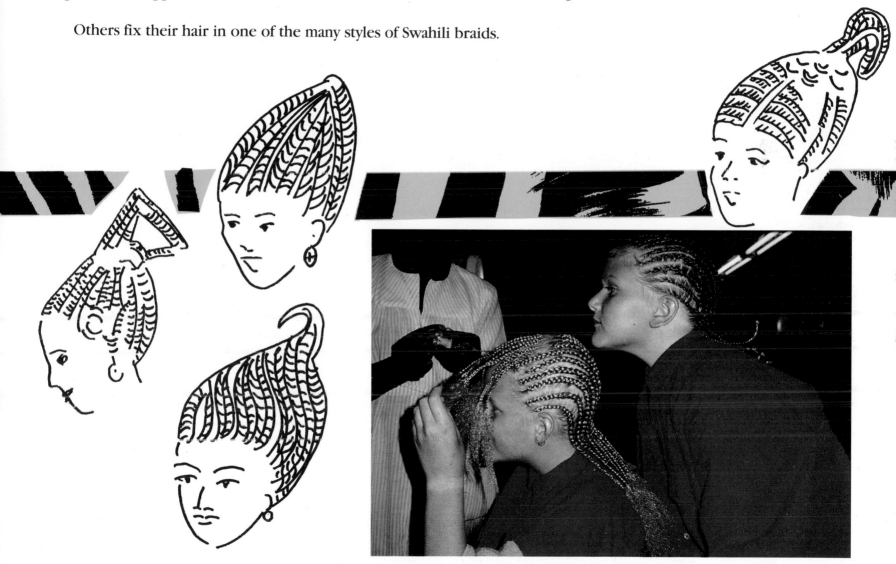

Plaiting takes hours, but, once braided, a style lasts for weeks.

Farmers raise many kinds of animals, but the most important are cows. They are like money. Both men and women own cattle, and traditionally the richest person has been the one who owned the most cows.

Tribes like the Rendille, Pokot, and Maasai are herders. They raise animals, too, but unlike farmers, herders don't live in one place. They move with their animals from place to place, to wherever they can find grass and water.

The Maasai are the most famous herders. They used to believe that God made all the cows in the world for them. They love their cows. They tie bells on them, shape their horns, and even write songs to them. Only on special occasions do Maasai butcher cattle for meat. For nourishment they drink cow's milk and, during dry seasons when the milk runs short, cow's blood. The cow is not killed to get the blood. With the tip of an arrow a small cut is made in a vein in the cow's neck. Blood drains into a container called a calabash, and the cut heals quickly.

Instead of playing cowboy or doctor like Robert does at home, Maasai boys play "herder". They learn to toss spears, play hide-and-seek, and pretend to fight off wild animals with sticks. When they're about six years old, the boys are allowed to take care of the family goats. As they get older, they're trusted to herd the cattle.

Because herders move from place to place, their houses have to be portable. They are built of branches plastered with mud and waterproofed with cow dung. When it's time to move, the women bundle up the branches and carry them on their backs to the next place they'll live. Young girls learn how to build houses, and when they play house, they actually build small real houses.

Children don't have toys bought from stores. When they play jacks, they play with rocks, and instead of tossing balls, they throw cow patties.

The girls make beautiful beaded necklaces and earrings for themselves and for their boyfriends. Each tribe has its own style of jewelry, and the pieces you wear depend on your age.

I was surprised to see teenage Maasai girls with shaved heads, while the teenage boys grow long hair and spend hours braiding it.

These young men wear fancy earrings, paint their bodies, and wear short skirts, too. But they are not sissies. The Maasai are the bravest and the most feared warriors in all Africa. A Maasai can kill an elephant or a lion with just a spear and a shield made of buffalo skin. They're great runners and athletes, too, and sometimes walk twenty-five miles a day.

Today the government is encouraging herders to switch the way they live, to stay in one place and to become farmers. I wonder how these proud people will live in a more modern, settled world.

In Kenya big families are important because everyone helps with the work. Some men have one wife, but others have two or three wives, and each wife has lots of children. I was puzzled how all these people could live together. It would be impossible in my house. The Kenyans have a great solution: they build a few separate small houses close together. Each wife has her own house where she lives with her children and small animals. A man with one wife may still have several buildings, one for the family and one for the kitchen.

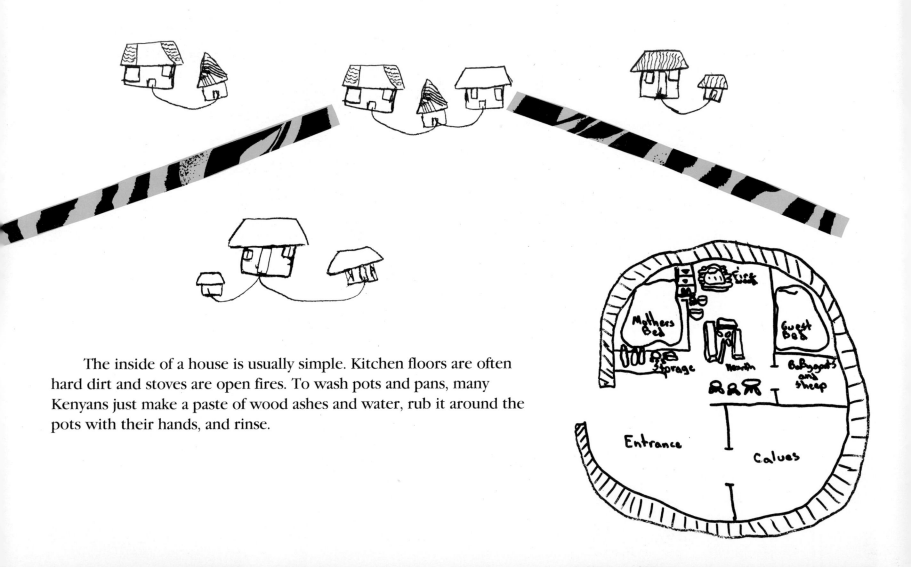

The inside of a house is usually simple. Kitchen floors are often hard dirt and stoves are open fires. To wash pots and pans, many Kenyans just make a paste of wood ashes and water, rub it around the pots with their hands, and rinse.

Women and girls have two of the hardest jobs. They sometimes walk for six hours a day to collect firewood and bring home water.

Learning to read and write is new for most Kenyans. In the past tribal languages were not written down. Grownups taught children their tribe's customs and beliefs through stories and songs. These are an important part of ceremonies to celebrate things like a harvest or becoming a grownup.

A Samburu boy must kill a lion to prove he's become a man. To celebrate his accomplishment and bravery, his people sing special chants, wrap his head like a lion's mane, and dance to clapping sticks.

As part of their ceremonies, some tribes paint their bodies,

some wear masks,

and some wear special clothes.

Members of the tribe don't just watch celebrations or sit and listen to the music. They join in by dancing, singing, playing an instrument or just clapping out the strong rhythms. Musical instruments are made from skin, horn, bone, wood, scrap metal, or whatever is available, so different tribes make and play different instruments. I heard lyres, reed flutes, thumb pianos,

and, the most famous, African drums.

Tribal traditions are still important, but today most children in Kenya go to school. If their parents can afford the fees and school uniforms, boys and girls start school when they're five years old.

Robert and I visited a family on their farm. Their house, like many in Kenya, didn't have electricity or running water. The children did their homework by the light from a kerosene lantern, and water was stored in a barrel in the front yard. Their life reminded me of stories my grandfather tells about his childhood, about helping with chores and working on a farm, about walking to school and getting up on cold mornings to build fires.

For a long time people have lived on the land where Kenya is today, but each tribe lived separately and had its own rules and customs. About a hundred years ago, the British bound the tribal lands together and made a British colony. In 1963 the people in the colony declared their freedom, and, for the first time, Kenya became a nation. It is such a young country that it has had only two presidents, Jomo Kenyatta and Daniel arap Moi. Their pictures are on Kenyan money.

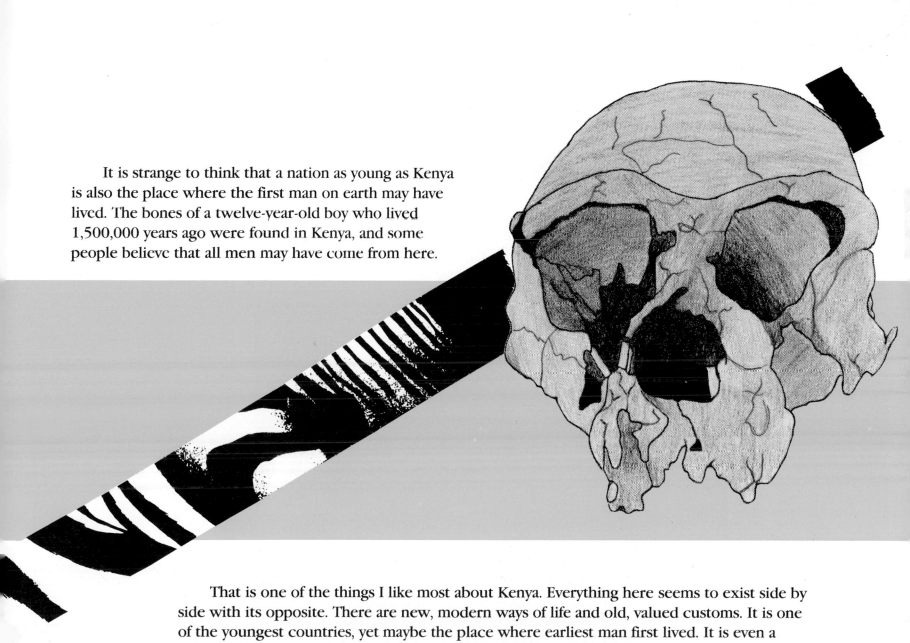

It is strange to think that a nation as young as Kenya is also the place where the first man on earth may have lived. The bones of a twelve-year-old boy who lived 1,500,000 years ago were found in Kenya, and some people believe that all men may have come from here.

That is one of the things I like most about Kenya. Everything here seems to exist side by side with its opposite. There are new, modern ways of life and old, valued customs. It is one of the youngest countries, yet maybe the place where earliest man first lived. It is even a country where you can find winter and summer at the same time.

Kenya is cut in two by an invisible line, the Equator. If you stand on one side of the Equator, it's winter. On the other side it's summer. But it doesn't matter what you call the season. Both sides are the same temperature. My mother suggested I try an interesting experiment. When I am south of the Equator and drain my bathtub, the water swirls clockwise. ↺ It's just the opposite on the north, the water circles counter-clockwise. ↻

Most countries along the Equator are hot, but not most of Kenya. A large part of the country is high and cool. I'd imagined jungles and instead found grasslands and mountains whose tops are capped wth snow year-round.

And animals, I knew there'd be animals, but I never dreamed there'd be this many. They roam wild and free, as if the whole earth were made for them.

To see and photograph the animals, you go on a safari. That's the Swahili word for journey. Dressed in jeans and armed with binoculars and cameras, not guns, we rode with a guide out into the fields.

Our van was open-topped, and sometimes it was so dusty we tied bandanas over our mouths and noses to help us breath. All the animals, even ones like baboons who seem friendly, are wild and can be dangerous. When you're out in the field, you stay inside your van.

At night we slept in tents, on cots draped with mosquito netting. It was dark and still. Then suddenly I'd hear rustling grass and a lion's roar.

Our guide told us fascinating things about the animals and taught us how to recognize some by their footprints.

A cheetah is the fastest animal and runs more than sixty miles an hour.

A hippopotamus is born underwater and has eyes on top of his head.

A zebra's stripes are like people's fingerprints; no two are the same.

A rhinoceros' horn is not bone. It's made of something like hair or fingernails stuck together.

An elephant uses his nose to carry trees and his ears for air-conditioning.

An ostrich is the biggest bird, but he can't fly.

A giraffe has a tongue that is 18″ long. He is the tallest animal on earth, yet he can hide in thornbushes from thin-skinned lions.

Our guide told me that there are more animals in Africa than anywhere else on earth.

Sometimes we'd go out in the early morning to photograph and sometimes in the late afternoon. There aren't many trees, and you can see for miles and miles. At first I had a hard time spotting all the animals, but, on each trip out of camp, my eyes grew more accustomed to looking and seeing.

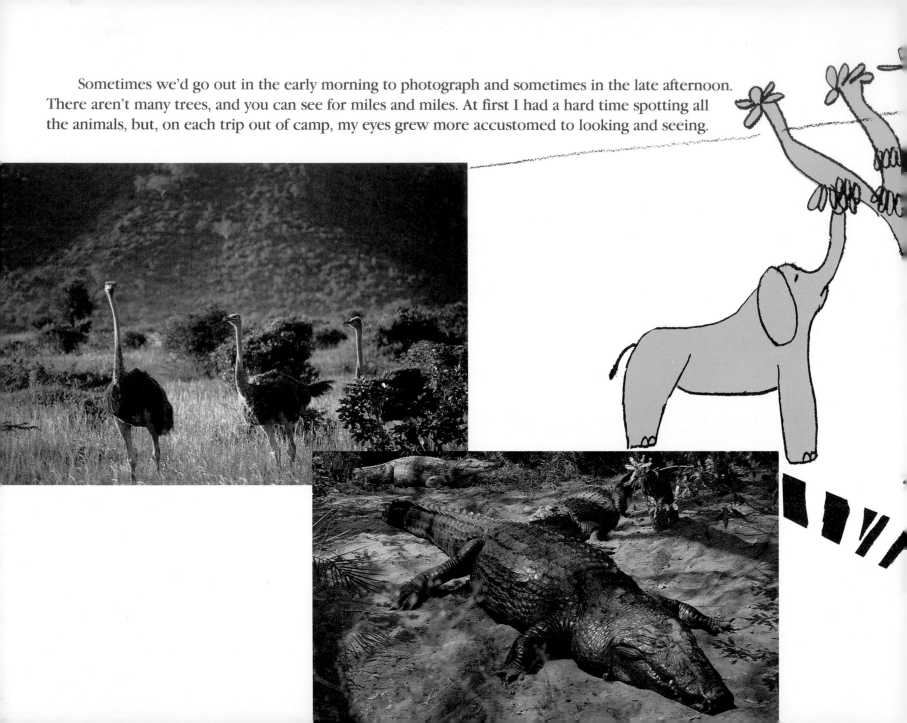

People come from all over the world to go on animal safaris. It's big business in Kenya. But there's also another big business that's thriving, the illegal slaughtering of animals. Poachers, some armed with machine guns, kill elephants for their tusks, rhinoceros for their horns, and leopards for their skins.

The animals face another danger. The population in Kenya is growing faster than in any other country, and animals are being squeezed into smaller spaces where it is harder to find food and water.

To protect the animals Kenya has set aside hundreds of square miles as National Parks. When you enter one on a safari, you're given a game card to check off all the animals you see.

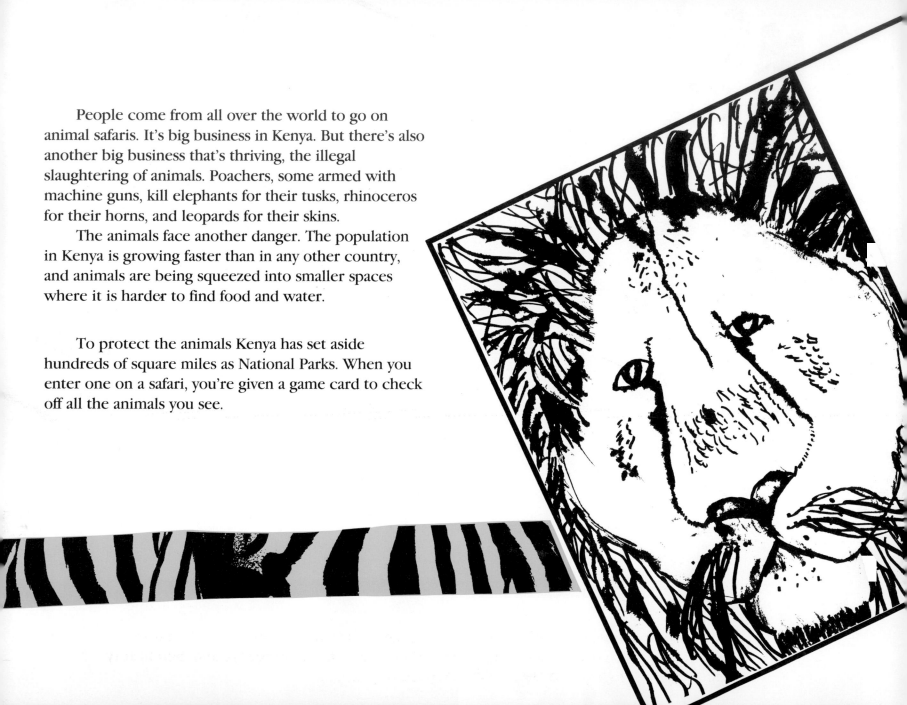

GAME RECORD

A CHECKLIST OF THE ANIMALS COMMONLY FOUND IN KENYA

PARK RESERVE _____

DATE _____

- [ ] Aardvark
- [ ] Aardwolf
- [ ] Baboon (Olive)
- [ ] Baboon (Yellow)
- [ ] Bat-eared Fox
- [ ] Bongo
- [ ] Buffalo
- [ ] Bush Baby*
- [ ] Bushbuck
- [ ] Bush-pig
- [ ] Caracal
- [ ] Cheetah
- [ ] Civet
- [ ] Crocodile
- [ ] Dikdik*
- [ ] Duiker (Bush)*
- [ ] Duiker (Red)
- [ ] Eland
- [ ] Elephant
- [ ] Genet cat*
- [ ] Gerenuk
- [ ] Giant Forest Hog
- [ ] Giraffe (Masai)
- [ ] Giraffe (Retic.)
- [ ] Golden cat
- [ ] Grant's Gazelle
- [ ] Hare
- [ ] Hartebeest*

- [ ] Hippopotamus
- [ ] Honey Badger
- [ ] Hunting Dog
- [ ] Hyaena (Spotted)
- [ ] Hyaena (Striped)
- [ ] Hyrax (Rock)
- [ ] Hyrax (Tree)
- [ ] Impala
- [ ] Jackals:
- [ ] Golden
- [ ] Silver-backed
- [ ] Side-striped
- [ ] Klipspringer
- [ ] Kudu (Greater)
- [ ] Kudu (Lesser)
- [ ] Leopard
- [ ] Lion
- [ ] Mongoose:*
- [ ] Banded
- [ ] Black-tipped
- [ ] Dwarf
- [ ] White-tailed
- [ ] Monitor Lizard
- [ ] Monkeys:*
- [ ] Colobus
- [ ] Patas
- [ ] Sykes
- [ ] Vervet

- [ ] Oribi
- [ ] Oryx *
- [ ] Otter
- [ ] Pangolin
- [ ] Porcupine
- [ ] Reedbuck*
- [ ] Rhinoceros (White)
- [ ] Rhinoceros (Black)
- [ ] Roan Antelope
- [ ] Sable Antelope
- [ ] Serval
- [ ] Sitatunga
- [ ] Spring Hare
- [ ] Squirrel (Bush)*
- [ ] Squirrel (Ground)
- [ ] Steinbok
- [ ] Suni
- [ ] Thomson's Gazelle
- [ ] Topi
- [ ] Warthog
- [ ] Waterbuck (Common)
- [ ] Waterbuck (Defassa)
- [ ] Wildcat
- [ ] Wildebeest
- [ ] Zebra (Burchell's)
- [ ] Zebra (Grevy's)
- [ ] Zorilla

* denotes existence of similar species or sub-species

It was exciting to check off how many I'd seen and to realize how much I'd learned about Kenya's animals. I'd also learned about her people, the way they live and their history, and I'd grown to love this fascinating, complicated place.

There is a special handshake that most Kenyans know:

You put your right hand on the inside of the other person's right elbow.
Then slide your hand down their arm and grab hands, like this.
Snap thumbs. That takes practice.
Then let go, snap your fingers, and smile.

When you shake hands like this, it means "friends for life!"

Kenya and its people had become my "friends for life!"

Kenyan food is delicious and fun to eat. I
think you'll like these recipes.

Spinach Stew

2 onions, finely chopped   1 t. salt
2 tomatoes, peeled & sliced   2 T oil
1 green bell pepper, chopped
2 lbs. fresh spinach, chopped, or 2 small pkgs. frozen spinach
2 chili peppers, or 1/2 t. cayenne pepper
4 T peanut butter

In a pot, saute onions in moderately hot oil. Stir in tomatoes and
green pepper. Add spinach, salt, and hot pepper. Cover, reduce heat,
and simmer 5 minutes. Thin peanut butter with a few T warm water.
Add to pot. Cook for 10-15 more minutes. Stir frequently. Add small
amounts of water as necessary to prevent burning.

Ugali

1 1/4 C white cornmeal
1 C milk
1 C water

Bring water to a boil. Gradually stir 3/4 C cornmeal into milk. Add
mixture to boiling water, stirring constantly. Cook for 4-5 minutes
while adding remaining cornmeal. Place in serving bowl and shape
into ball. With your fingers tear off a chunk and scoop up a bite of
stew. It's fun to eat without utensils!

Adapted from *Africa News Cookbook* with the permission of Africa
News Service and Viking Penguin, New York.